About the author

The mastermind behind 3rdCultureChildren Blog is a Foreign Service spouse, mother of three third-culture children, with an endless passion for discovering and learning new languages, cultures, traveling and photography.

Before joining the Foreign Service lifestyle, her background in Science and research, took her to understand that world is much more than the geographic and physical boundaries may display it.

She enjoys teaching, talking, and, as an avid blogger, sharing hers and her family's stories and lessons learned with other expat families. She has contributed her experiences to other blogs, online publications and, as a contributor to a recent book on expat resilience. Speaking as a foreign-born spouse, moving every couple of years, has become more intriguing than challenging.

As a traveling family, the Mirandas have lived in Mozambique, South Africa, Brazil, Bolivia, and during their work assignments, have traveled to England, Chile, USA and Swaziland. The author/blogger liked the idea of organizing not only her travel notes, but also providing resources for other parents, and encouraging an exchange of ideas through comments, questions and suggestions from viewers. The name for the blog came from the term itself: "Third Culture Children" are children whose parents come from distinct cultures, and grow up under a hybrid environment, experiencing diverse cultural growth. "The result of this transcontinental growth can never be taught or learned or fully understood by anyone who hasn't actually experienced it. The developing child takes the culture of their parent's passport country, or their first culture, to a foreign land.

The result is that the child (and later on, the adult) adopts the qualities of the Second Culture into their preexisting First Culture, creating a unique cultural perspective known as the Third Culture".

For an expat, a trailing spouse adapting to a second career, who is now raising three third-culture children, the titled seemed a natural fit!

The author is pleased to share with other expatriates, parents, and traveling families, not only the beauty and excitement of traveling, but also resources regarding languages, social and cultural adjustments, and our not-so-professional advice as "parents-on-the-go".

Recently, after talking with other 'trailing spouses', she came to the decision to 'share' a few of the op-pieces, posts and articles posted in the family blog in a book, using CreateShare[1], a new publishing resource already used by other aspiring authors within the foreign service community.

All the sections of this 'quasi-book' correspond to excerpts from the expat blog 3rdCultureChildren[2], the channel I discovered in 2011 and has become the outlet for my random thoughts on parenting while being a US Foreign Service trailing-spouse.

Like the op-pieces published in the blog, **view and opinions collected here are purely an expression of the author's personal thoughts, and do not reflect those of the US government, any of its agencies or officials. All information and comments presented here are in the public sphere.**

Thanks to an excellent team of bloggers[3], for sharing a good impression/definition of the term "third culture children", the implications, and the reason why the name of our family's travel blog was chosen.

The following excerpt comes from the public website Third Culture Blog – with an endless appreciation to its authors. They were the original inspiration and the reason this spouse 'blogs' about her family's challenges, difficulties and small victories, while experiencing the nomadic life of the Foreign Service.

---

[1] http://www.createspace.com
[2] http://www.3rdculturechildren.com
[3] http://www.thirdcultureblog.wordpress.com

The author's gratitude is expressed by the pleasure of sharing with readers:

*[Excerpt from Third Culture Blog[*Δ]] "The term Third Culture Kid (TCK) is one that has only recently begun to get a substantial amount of attention, despite its longstanding existence within the global community.*

It was coined in the 50's by Ruth Hill to describe those of us who were born in one country, or what I call "my parent's passport country," but have then proceeded to move in the formative years of our development to one or more "foreign" countries.

The result of this transcontinental growth is something spectacular, something that can never be taught or learned or fully understood by anyone who hasn't actually experienced it.

The developing child takes the culture of their parent's passport country, or their first culture, to a foreign land.

In that land, they interact with thousands of individuals who exist within a completely different culture, this being the Second Culture.

The result is that the child then adopts the qualities of the Second Culture into their preexisting First Culture, creating a unique cultural perspective known as the Third Culture.

[*Δ] http://www.thirdcultureblog.wordpress.com

The term TCK, though clearly using the word "kid," does not limit the group to only children.

Like everyone else, a TCK must one day grow up, and in doing so they become one of the most globally aware individuals on the planet.

They become an Adult Third Culture Kid (ATCK), possessing all the skills and qualities of a cultural melting-pot, but with the ability to view the world and the people in it with an eye that's shared by no one except other TCKs."

My personal expat tips for anyone following in our family's footsteps:

. Dream away. And dream big. Dream of traveling to unknown places, learning from new people, immersing into new cultures.

. Keep your expectations low. Many surprises should come your way if you're not waiting for anything!

. Be social. Be friendly. Be smart. Street Smart! Be conscious and be aware of your surroundings, as well. Teaching lessons come in different envelopes, sometimes, not-so-nice ones!

. Try to learn a new language, try to communicate with the locals and understand their stories and their culture. Communicate. Listen and be heard.

Attempt to comprehend the new country's traditions, faith, and fears.

Understand the harmonious relationship between the local community and Mother Nature.

Learn from their experiences and build your own story.

It's worthy every second we invest in!

How to prepare a 'serial traveler': Recipe, cooking times and serving suggestions.

How to serve a 'serial traveler':

Preparation Steps:

Make sure you've got all the ingredients handy.

Ensure their *good quality and origin*. When raising a child, remember to offer him/her a healthy dose of '*worldly experiences*': take them on field trips, sightseeing tours, museums, photo exhibits.

Share videos and tales from your own childhood.

Share with them your curiosity, your concerns, and your dreams.

Listen to their plans, their ambitions, and the fear of the unknown...

[Note from the Chef]

These are just suggestions for this dish. Alter as you please, adding or subtracting ingredients.

Come up with your own unique recipe and most important of all, have fun cooking!

Get the oven going: Take advantage of each and **every opportunity** to show your growing child that **the world is much more** than what they're gathering from social media tools.

Cooking and Serving:

Travel, go to places, and move.

By car, by bus, by train, by boat, on the back of a horse or camel.

Try flying, but also, try different transportation methods – **the stranger, the better**! Dealing with travel difficulties is part of the learning process, and overcoming challenges brings the experience to a whole new level.

Spend some time planning your trips. Imagine how it would be, what you'd do, who you'd encounter.

Dream about it. Enjoy the preparations and be ready to appreciate the reality, when the time comes.

Find **someone who shares your passions**, and share your life with him/her. *I did that, and have no regrets:* married another serial expat, and he's helped me raise our 3 little 'nomads'.

Try meeting new people. Chat with them. **Exchange stories**. Build new relationships.

Be yourself, be silly, and yet, be smart – care and attention are never excessive when moving out of one's comfort zone.

Try out new foods – it's an easy and fun way to immerse into the culture. Remember the smells and the tastes.

Take a *heart picture* of the dishes you're enjoying. Reserve for future use.

Check out city maps, newspapers, street posters. Don't know/don't speak the language?

Go for the pictures, the colors, the textures, the funny images and signs.

Remember: your friends or family back home are **living vicariously** through your travel experiences!

When traveling, visiting new places or renewing memories from old ones, take as many photos as possible.

Keep them handy for future use. Store in a tight container [*but please, not in the fridge!*]. You will surely need them for future recipes.

[*Note from the Chef*]

When checking out of hotels/hostels/B&Bs remember to always check under the beds for misplaced pieces of clothing, photo gear, and baby toys, lost socks and maybe *a kid or two*!

Recipe preparation and cooking times may vary. Season it to taste.

For some, it may take years and many mistakes/missteps before reaching the *'optimum point'*.

Be careful: **Try not to burn yourself**, but if it happens, make sure good friends and good memories to help you through the tough times surround you.

Use your best judgment when traveling, but once you begin **improving this recipe**, there's no way back – *you've certainly become a 'serial traveler'* like myself, my husband and the three little ones we haul around with! We can't really stay put for long...

Embracing Diversity as an Expat: Raising Children in the Foreign Service

The discussion on **social diversity** is not only part of our family's daily life, but it also tailors the way we are raising our children, and the way we would like them to understand and perceive their surroundings.

Being a *foreign-born spouse*, who has moved out of Brazil over a decade ago, constantly traveling because of work and family life, I had to learn early that, the need to **readjust and reinvent oneself** is a critical part of the adaptation process in a foreign country.

I'm also a parent, and often find myself trying to answer a few questions, to my own children, as well as, to other parents facing similar challenges:

"What can I do to help my children around the issue of diversity?"

And, in fact, *how ready is our society to embrace diversity?*

Life as an expat has shown me that we (parents) are the only *'constant'* on our children's lives.

Childhood friends **come and go**, depending on their parent's jobs. Schools change.

Countries, cultures, music, social patterns and expected behaviors last as long as one's post assignment does.

For a child, especially the young ones, parents are their **strongest link** to the concepts of '*reality*' and '*normalcy*'.

Over time, children will learn who they are and what to do through these experiences – absorbing a sense of their routines, traditions, languages, cultures, and national or racial identities – at their own pace, creating their very particular '*hybrid culture*', assuming their *own identity*, as unique social beings.

We are diverse, we speak different languages in our household, we come from distinct cultural and/or religious backgrounds... and our children could not be any different from that narrative.

Our children are coming up as divergent individuals, in a much richer way than we (parents) were brought up.

We are all very unique, and that notion needs to be reflected not only on the job represented by our officers (and their families) overseas, but also, through our own behavior as social creatures.

Diversity *brings innovation and creativity. It's important for us, parents, to add to our home environment, so it is reflective of other (cultural, racial, ethnic, family style) groups.*

It's critical to express **pride in our own heritage***. Building positive identities and the respect for differences, would mean inserting these concepts to the routine of children's everyday lives.*
I don't have answers for these questions, and maybe, secretly, would hope to find some from other expat/parents out there.

That said, *what is our role as parents? How could we help our children regarding diversity?*

One of the suggestions is that we need to be *constantly involved* in their lives.

Listening to their stories, learning about their ventures and challenges adjusting to new/unknown realities.

We need to devote a great deal of patience for establishing a healthy communication channel within our household, and between all the levels of our (expatriate) community; opportunities will present themselves at the school, at the work level, at social events where children may take part.

It's necessary to talk to our children about differences, in a very understanding and respectful way.

Let us be resourceful and take advantage of the diversity around us.

One of the advantages this life as expatriates offers to families is the possibility to enroll our children in international schools.

It's public knowledge that students who attend schools with a diverse population (student body, faculty, staff) are capable of developing an understanding of the perspectives of other children's backgrounds, learning to function in a multicultural, multiethnic environment.

All of us are born free of biases, (un) fortunately, we tend to learn them as we grow. Is it a totally negative aspect of our lives?

Could we turn our ability to make social judgments into a positive impacting tool? I'm aware that we [parents] are all seeking answers and/or suggestions, and in paving this track, I echo my voice with many other parental voices... *Who knows?*

Let the discussion begin!

Reflections on the expat life, inspired by Buckminster Fuller: "I am not a noun, I seem to be a verb"

This is a another post on my *'random thoughts'* about bringing our children up into this 'nomad world', especially when it comes to the diverse society they [children] are about to face. Any moment, now.

The discussion on social diversity is not only part of our family's daily life, but it also tailors the way we are raising our children, and the way we would like them to understand and perceive their surroundings.

For many children, expat life is an enriching, wonderful experience, but for many others, it is an unbelievably difficult time.

Much is gained — language, travel, worldview, and diversity – but there are very real losses — extended family, longtime friends, and a sense of belonging. Some of the losses are unrecognized and unacknowledged until later in life.

As parents of TCKs, my husband and I try to be sensitive to their particular situation.

Each child is different, and reacts to the up rootedness differently. Some are more sensitive, and others relish in it.

One thing we have always tried to be, however, is their anchor. Since their external life is in constant flux, we try to keep our family life constant and stable.

We try to have our own habits and traditions, which, as it turns out, are a bit of a blend between the countries we inhabit.

Yes, they [our kids] may be exotic to the kids around them, and again, each handles that differently.

One thrives on that, another cringes, but it is what it is.

We know that they would have a different perspective than we do as their parents.

Perhaps, the best way of handling the identity issue is to adopt the dictum of the late Buckminster Fuller: *"I am not a noun, I seem to be a verb..."*

Raising Children in the Foreign Service: A brief talk about Diversity

As noted by previous posts, nomadic/traveling children are highly exposed to diverse cultures, and we as parents should demonstrate why this is such an advantage to their own growth as human beings.

Building a culture of **diversity starts at home**, a literal reality for many State Department families.

We speak different languages, come from distinct cultural backgrounds, and practice different religions.

And yet in most cases, our children are growing up in a culturally richer environment than we (parents) were brought up. *Children in the Foreign Service tend to live the concept of diversity and its social implications – on a daily basis.*

That said, it is often necessary for us to question what is our role as parents in this process?

How can we assist our children regarding the issue of diversity?

It would appear as far as diversity is concerned, we need to be extra involved in their lives: listening to their stories, learning about their ventures and challenges adjusting to new, countries, discussing their questions and social frustrations, establishing a healthy communication channel, building positive identities and respect for differences.

Further, we should seek ways to insert these concepts into the routines of our children's everyday lives and help convince them through our actions, that a society without discrimination is possible.

It is critical for us parents and caretakers to develop 'cultural sensitivity' regarding our surroundings; otherwise, without specific cultural information, we may inadvertently promote practices and approaches that could counter other parents' efforts.

One great piece of advice I once received was to **"encourage your child's friendships with others across race, ethnicity, class, religious practices, background and ability."**

The more personal experiences children have with other groups, the easier it will be to dismiss stereotypes and misperceptions.

"Oso pardo, oso pardo, que ves ahi?" or Thoughts on the Creative Flow of a TCK

Although we were on family vacation, I'd asked our kids' teachers to give me some work sheets for their time off, in order to help them not forget about school, during their traveling days.

It may sound a bit "geeky", but hey, that's who we are, and that's what we believe it is the right thing to do... at least, for now.

Our oldest one is experiencing the challenges of "cursive letters". This morning I spend a few good hours with him – it's been raining, not a lot to do outside, and before we jumped into the *movie-marathon* mode, we did some 'homework' together.

And, actually, it turned out to be fun.

After we were done, it came to me the realization of how we're been raising our kids, immersed into **hybrid cultures**, always moving, always surrounded by **different languages,** doing homework in **Portuguese**, and proudly showing it to grandma, explaining her (in English) the task performed, and thanking grandpa for letting him borrow pencils and eraser, in **Spanish**...

It sure made me stop and think: is that how it's supposed to be? The children seem to adjust well to changes, **but how far is it possible to go**, without stretching it out?

The endless challenges of raising multilingual kids...

This is one of those days when I try to understand [and accept!] the decisions we've made for our lifestyle, the way we're raising our children, the kind of education parameters we [husband and I] need to make available to them.

As part of the educational tools my children need to be exposed to, are, for sure, the language/communication/social expression tools.

My children are surely enjoying their school break – another 2 full weeks to go, and they'll be back at a familiar environment – an international school, surrounded by Spanish speaking classmates, and other expats, mainly from neighboring South American countries, a few European reps, and the well-known US-American crowd.

All fun and games, until it came to reinforce the endless/continuous need for them [my kids] to keep speaking Portuguese at home.

Since I spend several hours at work, I'm not with them to 'remind' my little ones the importance of keeping up with 'mommy's language'.

They speak to the nanny in Spanish, to other American kids in English. The TV is mostly in English, with a few Spanish options.

I'm their only link to Portuguese, right now – and I feel it's my duty to stress the rule of 'if mom is home, you should only talk to her in Portuguese, as well as, to each other".

Guess what's happening? The rule is definitely off. We [parents] had it all planned out: our kick-off was the One Parent One Language (OPOL) method, where one parent speaks the minority language, which would be, in my case, Portuguese.

My husband would have the kids started in Spanish [his father's mother tongue], and gradually move on to English [husband's mother's tongue], as school moved on, and our children required a deeper knowledge of English.

We knew their brains are hard-wired for language acquisition and children up to three years old easily process both languages.

Our 3 children had an early 'linguistic' start – were introduced to different languages as early as their birthdate.

Soon, our family will be transitioning from our current Spanish-speaking setting, to a Brazilian Portuguese scenario. How would my kids [re] adapt?

What would be the social, emotional, psychological impacts this imminent move may bring? Only time will tell us.

Right now, it seems not to be working. Maybe, it's because we're tired at the end of the day?

Or because the kids see me talking to their dad in English; and to their nanny in Spanish, or Portuguese, they believe it's okay to leave aside the language of famous writer José Saramago, and completely pretend they don't know Portuguese [?]

Trouble with my culturally hybrid kids?

What do I mean by *trouble?*

Right now I'm simply trying to collect my thoughts into one piece, because attempting to answer this question has become my life task.

I joke with my three children that I was only a woman before they were brought into my life.

They made me turned into something completely different, the somehow scary concept of a parent.

Not easy to be a parent, and even harder the ongoing duty of (well) raising kids who are wholeheartedly part of a hybrid scenario.

The so-called hybrid culture, a moving creature, a living chimera who's not only part of their lives, but also defines who they (the children) are, the way they behave, how they interact with the (current) society, how they understand and express their feelings.

Our family is now experiencing the perks and wonders of our fourth work assignment[4], and we are again living in Brazil. This past week the children went to visit their new school, and participated in a short orientation activity with same-age/same grade kids. They were asked to introduce themselves, and mention where they were coming from, their previous school/country, stating their nationality.

My oldest was born in the US, and seems to have strong ties to the country thru sports, aligning him with the 'American' culture. He'd also tell you he's Brazilian – got a Brazilian-American mom and embraces the culture here. My surprise that day at school, came from my 1st-grader: when students originally from Brazil where called to stand up, she remained sited.

The same happened when US kids were called to introduce themselves.

Finally, when she heard, 'now, children from Africa', she jumped out of her seat, displaying a big and proud smile…

Yes, she was born in South Africa, while our family was leaving/working in Mozambique. She left the country before she turned 2.

But her allegiances to her 'African past' are remarkably strong – the culture, the music, the dances – she lives through the stories we tell her from the time our family spent there.

Who knows why? And, as long as she's happy, we're happy, despite our utterly lack of understanding.

Maybe, for now, the answers will just confuse us. Our focus needs to be directed to adapting, adjusting, and creating strategies to overcome upcoming challenges.

There is no time for worrying. The time now is devoted to looking for solutions – problems will always arrive, there is no need to seek them out…

---

[4] The Mirandas previous life/work assignments include La Paz, Bolivia (2012-14), Recife, Brazil (2010-12), Washington, DC (2008-09; 2003-06) and Maputo, Mozambique (2006-08)

As a parent, I've become aware of this 'chimera' my children represent.

Sometimes I feel I don't know them, and it's not their fault – I simply don't find the correct way to address their growing needs; how to respond to their sadness and anger; how to deal with their mood swings during the transitions, the constant moves, the new places, the losses of old friends.

Our family has relocated to our new post assignment – today marks the end of our second week in Brasilia. My children are comfortable with Portuguese, and have been able to make a few new friends during summer break.

They seem happy, they'd adjusting, and yet, they're struggling. I can tell from the little faces they're trying hard, they're no quitters, but sometimes the lack of (self) understanding turns into and default.

They look up to us (the parents) for answers we do not carry.

We knew it would be like this, we knew it wouldn't be easy, no transition is, but we're here for them, even though, my husband and I are still trying to figure things out: socially, emotionally.

For obvious reasons, our family dynamics feels a tad disjoint, but time and patience will hopefully be good allies throughout the process.

Time, patience, acceptance, and love – *our travel companions...*

Last thoughts: "The power of its name"

It came to life on March 2011, over three years ago...

And it's got a life of its own.

Some suspect it may have a mind of its own, as well.

Its words are provoking, but never arrogant.

Its shared thoughts often tend to bring out stimulating conversations.

But what is 'it'?

What's its name? Does it have any?

It's got an individual identity, and yet, it's got a social side. Quite a social face, some would state. It's public and yet, it's got its private features.

It's an experiment, a challenge, and a tale.

Others feed it and it feeds itself. It's lifeless and it's dynamic.

What's its name?

It's got one single title, which refers to the result of the modern transcontinental growth our society is witnessing; something spectacular, something that can never be taught or learned or fully understood by anyone who hasn't actually experienced it.

Its name is powerful and profound.

The name was given before its birth, while the female mastermind behind its creation, craved for a way to express the desire to share with the world her incomprehensible experiences living life as a nomad.

And while always a migrant, she raises worldly citizens under her wings...

Citizens that will display hybrid cultures, being the product of mixed backgrounds, histories, cultures and languages.

This self-maintained creature, repeatedly mentioned here, is an escape mechanism, a tool, and a voice to a parent's cries for advice.

*The voice given to this 'quasi-mythical' creation has a name, **Third Culture Children**, and through the lines of this blogging journey, the creature may have become as powerful as its creator; in an ironic and totally expected outcome.*

Its name brings many meanings, and the notion of children as an artifact of hybrid cultures goes beyond the physical explanations words may provide.

It's the name given to our family 'living journal', the blog from which the posts presented here were taken, represents the interface between the creator and its creation.

It's a living strategy to share thoughts, feelings and questions.

The name, although powerful as it should be, may never surpass the strength of the concept embedded on it – the definition of a child as a positive product of multiple influences, a TCK, a citizen of the world, ready for facing and overcoming life challenges.

A couple of years back when I began blogging, I decided to name this blog, representing/expressing what my kids are: the product of their mom and dad's hybrid/joined cultures.

Moving is part of our lives, *and was part of mine way before meeting the so-called 'best-half'.*

Through writing [and blogging] I'm 'mapping out my life', the moves I've endured as a nomad child back in Brazil, as well as the ones leading me to a new path as an expat, mother and 'trailing spouse'...

Thank you!

RM

www.ingramcontent.com/pod-product-compliance
Lightning Source LLC
Chambersburg PA
CBHW052357010625
27565CB00013B/1196